SECOND BLOOM

The Poiema Poetry Series

Poems are windows into worlds; windows into beauty, goodness, and truth; windows into understandings that won't twist themselves into tidy dogmatic statements; windows into experiences. We can do more than merely peer into such windows; with a little effort we can fling open the casements, and leap over the sills into the heart of these worlds. We are also led into familiar places of hurt, confusion, and disappointment, but we arrive in the poet's company. Poetry is a partnership between poet and reader, seeking together to gain something of value—to get at something important.

Ephesians 2:10 says, "We are God's workmanship . . ." *poiema* in Greek— the thing that has been made, the masterpiece, the poem. The Poiema Poetry Series presents the work of gifted poets who take Christian faith seriously, and demonstrate in whose image we have been made through their creativity and craftsmanship.

These poets are recent participants in the ancient tradition of David, Asaph, Isaiah, and John the Revelator. The thread can be followed through the centuries—through the diverse poetic visions of Dante, Bernard of Clairvaux, Donne, Herbert, Milton, Hopkins, Eliot, R. S. Thomas, and Denise Levertov—down to the poet whose work is in your hand. With the selection of this volume you are entering this enduring tradition, and as a reader contributing to it.

—D.S. Martin
Series Editor

Second Bloom

Poems

ANYA KRUGOVOY SILVER

CASCADE *Books* · Eugene, Oregon

SECOND BLOOM
Poems

Cascade Books
An Imprint of Wipf and Stock Publishers
199 W. 8th Ave., Suite 3
Eugene, OR 97401

www.wipfandstock.com

PAPERBACK ISBN: 978-1-5326-3007-1
HARDCOVER ISBN: 978-1-5326-3009-5
EBOOK ISBN: 978-1-5326-3008-8

Cataloguing-in-Publication data:

Names: Silver, Anya Krugovoy

Title: Second bloom / Anya Krugovoy Silver.

Description: Eugene, OR: Cascade Books 2017 | Series: The Poiema Poetry Series.

Identifiers: ISBN 978-1-5326-3007-1 (paperback) | ISBN 978-1-5326-3009-5 (hardcover) | ISBN 978-1-5326-3008-8 (ebook)

Subjects: LCSH:

Classification: XV0000 X00 2017 (paperback) | XV0000 (ebook)

Manufactured in the U.S.A.   08/10/17

For Andrew and Noah,
my beloveds

*"Sorrow is better than laughter, for by sadness of countenance
the heart is made glad."*
—ECCLESIASTES 7: 3

*"Let my poem be as transparent as a windowpane
Against which a straying bee hits its head."*
—ANNA KAMIEŃSKA

Contents

I

Cape May at Dusk

At the cape, I stood alone on a platform
watching swans gather, mallards and herons,
and below me, a single rabbit, feeding itself
in the twilight on soft, newly mown grass.
I don't know why I'm still alive.
I don't know how a line of poetry
sometimes loses itself and finds me.
I don't understand why my body is drawn
to the marshes, or to the surf dragging
itself away from the shore.
Why does memory cling to the briny air,
settling in my hair like the sandy wind?
I've wasted so many days in half-life—
shopping, pop music, magazines.
I should have been thinking of holiness
and trying to find it—even on these humid
afternoons when there's space for image
but the air is too dense to grasp the form.
I stand and watch the rabbit, a lean
wild one, as it attends to its hunger,
till a little girl comes stomping over,
shrieking, and it disappears in the wild roses.

Exile

Lately, I've wanted to be alone.
To leave home with nothing
but a few books and my favorite shoes.
I'd like to live in the mountains,
but pleasantly, with a broad bed
and cheese and bread for my board.
No computers, no commute.
Just to sit with a pen (like now)
writing honest lines of poetry
that no one is likely to read.
Simple, harmless, with words and firs
for company, some music—
at night, the wind at the shutters,
in times of sorrow, the Psalms.

A Boy Stands Up During Supper

A church in the East is abandoned.
First, rain and snow breach the roof,
the ceiling leaks and slumps, then buckles
in great plaster sheets, shattered and dusty.
Now all manner of rust and rot can enter,
weeds and moss growing between the pews.
Worms in the wood, an aisle of mulch,
an altar of dandelions, nests, and seed.
The church fails board by board,
jagged window by jagged window
through which bees travel unimpeded.
It whistles and groans, this dying church.
When a boy tries to find it, it's gone.
His mother collapsed from the inside out,
her heart and lungs accumulating liquid
until there was too much to sieve,
and she told her grieving son, "Go East,"
not knowing the church he sought was a dream,
a cracked dish, a syringe of morphine.

Return

When he returned home after many years,
an enormous oak had split his house in two,
its trunk growing right through the center hall.
Though there was nobody living in the tilting
rooms, he recognized some simple objects:
a milk jug once filled with daisies, a single shoe.
Where a mirror had dangled, a darkened oval
remained on the wall. No bark, no call, no singing.
But though he didn't understand what he saw,
he knew the tree, broad and green, was a blessing.

Demeter Mourns the Sisters

As though grief were not enough,
I must write of it. Ulcerous earth
demands my black-seeded poppies.
Women's names frame ebony October:
Maria, Julie, Ishiuan, Anne.

I want to recast them as verbs,
sink them like bulbs, latent but alive,
and await their allium globes
once the shriving is over.

But I don't bear false hopes.
My gift to the mourning is winter.
Leaflessness winnows pain.
Imagine the trees bare for your sake,
branches click clacking in the wind
like fluid-filled lungs wheezing air.

Follow my shadow. Pluck the bitter
herbs at your feet, then baste
with them a steaming bowl of tubers.

Almond Blossoms

On night shift in the ICU,
Rebecca tends to the sickest
patients, the ones subdued
on morphine and likely to die.
When she's free, she drives
the backroads of California,
photographing almond trees.
Joy is a gift not given to all.
In pain, it's evasive as a squirrel.
My friend, who can no longer lift
her head, her neck bowed down
with blistered tumors, tells me
I'm tired of fighting the beast.
So I clasp happiness while it exists.
Almond crowns bloom so briefly.
One day they're white, the next, green.
Rebecca works in the fluorescent night.
In the afternoons, she photographs
the clapping, breathing trees.

There Are Times

Today, when I could be writing,
I sit waiting for a nurse to access me
(that is, puncture me with a needle).
I cannot work because of the talk,
the cold room, the television's jabber.
The microwave smells of grease and burn.
I want words, but my mind stalls.
Too much blabbering, too many bells.
Staring into the IV's neutral blue gaze,
I search for an apt metaphor for poetry:
my burning eye, my bride, my thread.
I'm not sure whether I've given up
on words, or whether they've deserted me.
I'm in the sea, there's no comfort
in the tides, my spit tastes of saline.

Department Meeting

Tragedy won't stop the world's drone.
Weekly meetings continue, typed agendas
shuffled on the table like the Dead Sea's tides.
Illness remains impolite among colleagues.
When I mention cancer, the eyes around me lower.
The woman to my right pushes up her glasses.
The woman to my left nods vaguely, pen hovering.
Then all attention turns to questions of the budget.
Outside the window, boughs rustle pointlessly.
Everyone agrees that Shakespeare is still relevant.
The eyelet of a shoe imperceptibly loosens
from its stitching, the unraveling begun in earnest.
Even words seem to lose their stickiness and fall,
sickly, from the ceiling tiles. Only I notice them.
Very slowly, so as not to make anyone nervous,
I shake my head and x's drop from my hair.

To a Healthy Friend

What is suffering but tedium?
Picking pebbles from lentils,
numb feet stumbling to the bathroom,
hoping to make it to the toilet on time.
But off go the panties to be scrubbed.
We're gross and boring, and if no one wants to listen,
I don't blame them. I was that way, too.
Do you think I want your dish-rag pity
wrung all over my lap? Your cat eye comfort?
Everyone dies. That's supposed to lift me
to my toes and spin my final *pas de deux*?
Tell you what. Leave the suffering to us.
You're not invited. Eat pound cake
till your buckle bursts. Lose everything.

How to Talk to a Sick Woman

Do not make me your nightmare.
Refrain from invoking me among
the *A,B,C's of your fear.*
(There's no cure, it's true. That's why
I'm so blue.)
I'm not your *it could be worse*
or proof of the smallness of your woes.
My bad luck is not your good luck.
(And by the way, fuck you.)
Your pity, though meant to be kind,
undoes me. I find it dreary.
Nor am I the Madonna of cancer,
your bow-arched Amazon. Make me your inspiration
if you like, but I don't deserve praise.
My days are as ordinary as yours.
And when I die, what will you do?
You'll have lost your light-strung Santos.
Cede me back my story.
My veins spout open, then close like magic.
I don't dread death more than you do.
Only I get to say I'm tragic.

Me, Us

Today, I saw a hawk clutching
a mourning dove in its talons.
The ground was a white mess
of clawed feathers—a struggle.
And yesterday, Nathalie died.
Every death, a slap that knocks
me backwards. Me, us.
I lose myself in the others.
We hope, we trust; death's
barbed nail on our nape
still surprises us.

The Wild Swan Geese

They descend suddenly, a great flock
on their razored feathers, squawking, flapping
toward us, their eyes black and implacable,
their beaks scissoring the air as they shriek.
We run together, pushing through the woods,
holding hands, but even so, some of us stumble.
We don't look back. The geese come for the fallen.
The farther we run, the muddier the soil,
the faster they fly—their cries discordant keys
struck over and over on a rotten piano.
We love each other, but no one, no one, can save us
from the geese, which are toothed and ruthless.
Oh, that woman was so close to me, but she's dropped
to the ground. I watch the geese wheel her away.

Things That Do Not Fade

"I love time and sense and fading things and things that do not fade."

–Emily Dickinson

It's no longer possible, I'm told by a poet,
to symbolize death with falling leaves.
Yet how to look at maples, reddening
by the road, then dwindling and drifting,
without these thoughts of death in mind?
And how could I love this evening,
this painless evening, sheer blue gauze
twisted in and around a woman's braids,
without knowing that one windy storm
could shear the trees of all color?

Kelly is dying, she knows it and so do I,
though she won't use the word, but sleeps
most of the day and eats when she's able.
Her face a round, steroidal apple.

So hard to love time, its creeping hunger.
I'd like to leave that love for others.
But this gold mulch, this crumpling twilight.

Something Understood

We were talking about beauty, three women and I,
and the oldest among us, still lovely in face,
told another, *You should go on the cancer diet.*
It's the best way to lose weight. And like a wisp,
I rose from the gossip and took flight;
my breath carried me to heights hidden
behind the clouds of that dark day, above birds
crowding in great black flocks in the park.
I knew I had entered forever the world of the ill.
I would never return to that other, open life
of carefree women peeling tangerines.
Sheared off, I was, like the umbilical cord
of my friend's newborn, slashed by her hip bone
as he was pushed too early into a cold birth.

Grape Popsicle

No food for three days. Total bowel rest.
My pancreas has turned anarchist, an egg
and soup leaving me unable to walk.
Lying in the hospital bed, I watch commercials
for food, plan my meals, name the snacks
I miss most—apples, bagels, popcorn.
Only electrolytes, pumped through an IV,
are permitted, and, catheterized, my urine
drips into a little bag to be measured.
There is nothing I want more than mouth-
fuls of whipped cream, syrupy flan, yellow
cake smeared with raspberry jam.
Lying on the slippery mattress, I smell
the staff's food from their station—
fried, sauced, roasted, broiled.
The fourth day, a nurse pulls out the catheter.
I lift, from the tray before me, something I
would never buy—a grape popsicle,
the color of a crayon, in a soggy white wrapper.
I run my tongue along the ice-furred top.
Nothing has ever tasted so good!
Purple syrup, unnaturally sweet.
Impatient, I bite off chunks, feel the cold
burn as I let it melt before I swallow.

Al-Quddus

One of the ninety-nine names of Allah

Yours is the name of God that comes most easily to me—
God holy, pure, perfect as geometry, *that which is set apart.*
God to whom I pray, though I deserve no favors.
And would you, Al-Quddus, whom I simply call God, Lord,
bargain with my heart for life? As other from human as ether,
would you turn your non-self, whole self, toward my voice?
I stand in a circle of women chanting your name.
No—begging your name. Swimming in your strange indigo.
Our voices ring out like copper prayer bowls.
Unblemished one, breathe yourself into my spoiled body,
my body bitter as rind, which I am trying so hard to love,
and like steam, draw out the stains in my bones and lungs.
Let me feel whatever it is you are (for I can never know).
Heal me.

Poetry Belongs to the Dying

We crouch together in a cellar.
The air stinks of pus and disinfectant.
Bombs strafe the floors above us.
We're hidden, but not safe.

Each week, we stack the dead,
their veins, snapped blue threads.
(Strangely, people outside
ignore the demolition.)

When someone dies, the word passes
from one marked tongue to another—
we pull the dusty raven feathers
from each other's sprung throats.

Even when we're gagging sick,
our bodies stalks, awaiting mowing,
we stuff pill bottles with words.
We hold the secret to everything.

Getting Used To It

I lie when I say it never gets easier.
It does: the shock of death rusts,
like a car engine left in the rain too long.
After Kate died, I stopped reading obituaries,
no longer made friends whom I'd probably lose.
If I look away from illness, it's easier to pretend
it isn't stowed among the hamper's dirty clothes,
or nibbling at the bag of dry dog food, until one night
a hole releases the kibbles all over the floor.
Hearing about death is like eating salsa—
at first, you order it mild, then go spicier
and spicier. Finally, not even the hottest pepper,
bitten right through the middle, is likely to make you cry.

II

First Advent

Bury her under strawberries.
That girl never wed,
bury her too high for floods.
Mother, what well
will you descend?
What webs pin you to the world
now? Only others' hands,
words a small black blot
where I've held the pen too long.
Almost Christmas, the solstice
about to tip toward the sun.
No strawberries this season.
Cover her bed with hollies:
unyielding merciless red.

Second Advent

Red bows on lamp posts,
blood clot a hibiscus in your brain,
petals spreading in your cerebral cortex.

The neurosurgeon drills a hole
in your skull to relieve the pressure,
then gouges tumors from your tissues.

I imagine your head alit with aura—
blue, rivering corona. Death exists,
but it has not yet overcome you.

The solstice gathers its lunar bonfire.
Your skull is sutured and swaddled.
You fall asleep, you wake, it's Sunday.

The second candle burns in its greens.

In memory of Ishiuan Hargrove

Third Advent

"In this way Our Lord Jesus Christ, the spiritual unicorn,
descended into the womb of the Virgin, and through her took
on human flesh."

-*Physiologus* (2nd-4th century)

Night slants toward the solstice,
the lunar shutters preparing to open,
to welcome the straying sun's return.
Already, the third Advent has flamed
and been extinguished in its wreath.

This winter, I turn forty-eight.
Another year has grown to fullness,
round like the *Lebkuchen* that nuns
bake at Christmas on communion wafers,
moon-shaped biscuits, dark and spiced.

Cancer has not yet killed me.
I have drunk again from the unicorn's
horn; it has healed me, for now,
as in generations past. God kicks
against the rocking womb, waiting.

Fourth Advent

On Sunday, I lie beside a friend in bed,
weeping, because she doesn't want *a better place.*
How bleak the next life to her grieving sons,
who need their mother here, on earth—
her silly wigs, her marathons, her fingers
deftly pinching dumplings for the feast.
For our sins, it's said that Christ was born.
The manger's set up in the church,
my friend sleeps through her steroid pills.
The nights grow still. We wait, Emmanuel.
Merciful one, begotten of woman, understand
how difficult it is to trust that you are kind.

All You Souls

Ale goldens my glass with the slow, sweet tones
of bourbon-soaked oak chips and vanilla.

It's the evening of the winter solstice.
Night has tipped each drop from its bottle,

leaving a slit through which the sun will pour,
bit by bit, through winter's dark months.

On this thin night, doors open for the dead.
There's a liquid humming beneath the floor.

All you souls, join me to toast the coming year,
merry among the colored lights and balsam.

Christmas Eve

Tonight, I imagine Bethlehem—
not the actual city, but the town in the hymn,
a village I've seen on Advent calendars,
numbered windows opening onto a lit candle,
candied fruit, spinning top, singing angel.
I enter the propped-up paper landscape,
my footsteps the only crunch on glitter snow,
and find a tiny church where rows of candles
flicker all night long, and Mary cradles her son.
In a nook, I rest, remembering the trees
of my childhood, bright as prophets' tongues.
The air is orange-steeped. Everyone I've lost is here.
We're bound together in a dreamless sleep.

My Mother Plays a Christmas Carol

I've never heard my mother play piano.
Yet there she sits, Christmas carols keyed
from her fine, eighty-year-old fingers.
I only played for three years, she says,
but it stays in your mind like typing.
A song she hasn't sung in decades returns to mind:
Es Wird Schon Glei Dumpa.
                    Darkness is dropping.
The notes loop her back to childhood
in Switzerland, the war just over. No toys
for Christmas, just an orange and tin of biscuits.
It's snowing in Basel, the bridges silently icing.
My dead Grannie stands in the kitchen doorway,
younger than I am now, not knowing that I
will inherit her face, and her beads of white coral.

Eating Baklava on New Year's Eve

The little honeyed manuscript
on my plate drips stickily
as I turn its leaves with my fork.
There must be a blessing here:
its three corners Trinitarian,
phyllo dough a Nativity swaddle.
Thirty-three layers, wispy petals,
Christ's life and death consumed
with each bite of golden parchment.
The old year sheds its final page
from the stitching, the new year splits ajar—
shatter of glass, clatter of noisemakers,
dust and hoofbeats beneath the star.

Colloquy

from the Colloquy *of Aelfric (955-c. 1010)*

i. Fisherman

Master: Would you catch a whale?
Fisherman: No.
Master: Why?
Fisherman: Because it is a dangerous thing to catch a whale.

How do you catch a whale?
No net you knit is strong enough
to contain it, no hook you fashion
strong enough to tug it toward you.
With what would you lure it?
It needs nothing you offer,
neither can force bring it to you alive.
What, then, can be said to catch
a whale? Only the barnacle,
floating eyeless, unknowing.
The best way is to wait
until the whale comes close,
and fling yourself on its breaching back.
The best way to catch a whale
is to dig in, to root, to ride
with it the deep down tides,
listening to its unfathomable song.

ii. Ploughman

Master: Can you tell us, ploughman, how you do your work?

Ploughman: Master, I have to work so very hard. I go out at the crack of dawn to drive the oxen to the field and yoke them to the plough. I must plough a whole field or more for the whole day.

To wake each morning, too early,
for the feeding of dumb animals,
for the buckled harness and yoke.
To lumber back and forth along long furrows,
the syllabic tramp of boots, the turning
over of dense and weedy earth, inky black.
And afterwards, to clean the stable, too,
carry out the wet and stinking dung.
Imagine the trudge, the hours whittled,
the work his bonded life requires.
His lord's laborer, readying the field,
sowing, bundling the sweet hay.
The day to day offering, too, of mind—
the skipping plough and the leaping line.

iii. Salter

Master: Salter, how does your craft benefit us?

Salter: Everyone benefits a great deal from my skill. No one enjoys his break-
fast or dinner unless my skill is present in it. Indeed, all the butter and
cheese would go bad unless I looked after it.

O Lord, our God,
how delicious is your name!
And glad is everyone who recognizes
    in the world the works of your fingers.

Salter, you shall eat fish in summer,
    and in autumn, the garden's bitter greens.
You will brine the harvest for winter's broth.
And in spring, you will sprinkle salt and herbs
    on the eggs of your fruitful hens.

The treasures of the mines and the seas
    will be precious to you, and the trees and vines.
You will season all of God's creation with joy.
Order and radiance will follow your footsteps.

The Lord will bless those who cure,
    who sow the tears of the sorrowful and harvest
        the feathered sheaves of peace.
Blessed are those who preserve the earth,
    for they shall be preserved.

iv. Birdcatcher

Master: How do you feed your falcons?

*Bird catcher: In winter, they feed both themselves and me, but in the spring, I
    set them free to fly away to the woods, and in the autumn, I catch young
    birds and tame them.*

The lucky falcons are those I catch.
They learn the joy of being trained,
of answering to a name, a whistle
that calls them over distances,
and a wrist that holds their weight.
From thousands of nests, they are chosen.
In winter's wastes, they no longer wander.

But in restless spring, when drawn
to nests among the rocks, to hares
in greening woods, and the preen
and dance of feathers, their chained
talons chafe and ache, and the safe
perch ensnares. Then, in pity, I set
them free, for their own, pitiless, sake.

v. Merchant

Teacher: What have you to tell us, merchant?

Merchant: I embark on board ship with my wares and I sail over remote seas, sell my wares and buy precious objects that are unknown in this country. I bring these things to you over the sea enduring great danger and shipwreck. I bring purple cloth and silk, precious stones and gold, various sorts of clothes and dyes, wine and oil.

Come with me to his shop, come with your empty bags.
Much of what you miss you'll find there.
Bind amber-beaded silver round your arms,
Lamb's wool dyed wine-dark around your neck.
Brass bells, pearled slippers, ebony bowls,
candles that weep with the spice of cloves.
If you're hungry, there's bread for the taking,
there's oil, and fruit that falls from the pit.
If you need to sit, there are pillows and chairs.
Needles for mending, ointment for scars.
There are skulls, and ash, and stumble stones.
There are boxes you'd better not touch.
You'll find words to pin to your fraying hems,
to thread in the braids of your hair.

Lenten Crocuses

A burst of crocus
in the oak's roots opens
one Sunday like a little choir.
Purple, as befits the hours—
shrouded cross, altar cloths.
All winter, their bulbs spread,
pushing hard against the soil.
Their saffron pollen stains,
smearing the probing finger.
They're Easter before Easter,
plenty while fasting, open tomb.
Their petals, candled windows.
They're Hosannas, vessels
that draw in weak sun, cupping
its rays in the last days of dark.

Holy Saturday, 1945

It was for you, Maria Skobsova,
that Mozart wrote his Requiem.
Bolshevik nun, instead of celebrating
the funeral of Christ, you walked
into the gas chamber at Ravensbrück
in place of another woman.
Instead of trailing the coffin
around the church, you claimed
a place in the line entering hell.
It was for you, Maria Skobsova,
that Mozart fainted in the writing
of his mass, *Let them, Lord, pass.*
All work remains unfinished:
the composer's delirious lines,
the forging of baptismal certificates
in your Parisian convent, the censing
of the church on Holy Saturday.
Instead of incense, fumes of Zyclon B
haloed the shorn heads of the dying.
No beaded shrouds for Mozart's
common grave, for your grey smoke.
Give thanks to the Lord, we sing.
for he is good: for his mercy endures forever.

The Empty Tomb

Mary's brave enough to lean inside.
No corpse, no reek, no bloated face,
her rabbi's flayed and hammered body gone.
The angels offer her no comfort.
Woman, why are you weeping? they ask,
curiously, as though she were a child.
Woman, why are you weeping? Jesus asks.

It's Christ re-bodied, and all is bells and joy.
We hug the peace, stamp our feet, sing
Christ is risen from the dead! Trampling
down death by death! Then knock eggs,
cave-rolled rocks, against each other.

So difficult, though, to see beyond the tomb.
Those who've peered inside the dark room
understand—the absence there, the hollow
chest, the stitched-shut mouth, the way
that letters stop, and phone calls too,
an abscess winding from the wound.

Easter Sunday

Isaiah 42:3

Easter morning, a yellow sheath dress and an IV bruise,
my inner arm gummy with surgical tape.
A dimly burning wick He will not extinguish. . .

Today's a day for joy, for wreathing the cross
with azaleas, for white wine in the communion
cup instead of red.

And after the benediction, the shouts of children
searching for eggs in the labyrinth, candy
cradled among the stones.

My son flashes a golden egg in his palm, his gesture
like that of Mary Magdalene, the egg in her hand
flushing from white to crimson.

Miracle of pigment, vein, blood, and resurrection.
Of each cell in its transformations.

III

Psalm 137 for Noah

Come darling, sit by my side and weep.
I have no lyre, no melodious voice or chant.
I meditate on the Zion I could never grant you.
My son, my roe deer, my rock-rent stream.
My honeysuckle, my salt, my golden spear.
Forgive me your birth in this strange land.
I wanted your infant caresses, your fists clasped
round my neck. I craved you, though you were born
in the wake of my illness, my dim prognosis.
I was selfish: I willed you this woe, this world.
You inherited exile for my sake.

Pedals

On the corner of Cherry Street and Vine,
the dump truck operator notices my son
and me watching from the sidewalk,
invites us to climb in the cab for a ride.
My four-year-old helps push the levers
up and down, observing how the shovel
digs up dirt and rocks, metal teeth grinding
the hard red earth, widening and deepening the hole.
My daughter passed when she was about your son's age,
the man says, suddenly. *Leukemia. A fighter.*
They have the same light brown hair.
Then he changes the subject, points out the pedals,
how one pedal makes the truck move forward,
and the other makes it stop.

Fall Festival

They strapped us in belts.
And then we swung up, up, up,
and plunged down, three times
round to the right, three times
to the left, each drop a scream
like an old factory steam whistle
blowing time. *We're all gonna die!*
the boy beside me bawled
as the gears hauled us higher
than century-old magnolias.
My son hooded his head
and dug it in my shoulder,
waiting for the ride to be over.
And then it was—so suddenly.
Gradually, he unbent his back
and relaxed his clenched face,
and we walked together
into the crowds, the sounds
of shrieking all around us,
along with bells, horns, and bands,
but the crazy motions over now,
as I held tight his sweating hand.

for Noah

Inauguration

The augurs have retreated
to the temples and caves of history.
Nobody, now, watches the birds'
turning in flight, their wind-traceries,
or listens to the tempo of their songs.
Nobody examines for omens the seeds
and bones left in their droppings,
leaving the will of the gods mute.
The word-grinders smile as they speak
from podiums, and the oracles babble.
Goldfinches squawk, too small for their crowns.
Somebody should call the ravens.
Call them back to the cliffs, the mounds, the sea.
The future unwinds around us, sheer and black.

Kharkov, 1933

In 1933, when he was almost starving,
my father knocked a loaf of bread
from an old woman's hands, and ran.
She had her revenge, though,
visiting him night after night
as he lay dying. *She's forgiven you*,
I kept telling him, but he wasn't sure.
In dreams, he saved her dinner.
Here, eat this, my father pleaded,
offering his uneaten roll to the woman,
who didn't respond, who neither
opened her mouth nor bared her teeth.

A Walk in November

My father believed that autumn
is the poet's season, and recited Pushkin,
Poetry awakens in me then.
One day, he wanted to walk together.
I found excuses, wouldn't be persuaded
by the sunset of maples up and down the street.
He pantomimed falling leaves with his hands.
I didn't want to hear his reveries.
Ah well, he shrugged, *I did my best,*
then started on his daily stroll alone.
Whenever we lost something in our home,
my parents joked that Pushkin took it.
Too late now to put aside my book
and follow him outdoors that afternoon.
My father's voice has been misplaced.
Pushkin strode the wooden floors.

In memory of George Krugovoy

Envying the Amish

We knew not to take their photographs,
but how my sister and I stared at girls
in long purple dresses with wrist sleeves
even in hot Lancaster County summers.
Once, we visited a model Amish house—
set up for tourists like ourselves—
where the guide held up a small box:
"When an Amish woman travels, this case
will hold all she needs."
The teen behind me gawked:
"My makeup wouldn't even fit in there."
I cringed that the quiet guide had heard,
and thought, how relieved a girl must feel
with so little burden, the same lightness
I imagined children feeling as they swung
on long ropes from trees, ignoring our car
as we slowed to watch them play.
I couldn't understand that balance—
to be so earth-bound,
pinned to a single place like identical dresses
on the line, and at the same time so free
that if there were a fire, one wouldn't worry,
like I did, about which outfit to save.

Girl Braiding Her Hair

Albert Anker (1887)

A girl plaits her hair, a bowl of water
and an open book on the table beside her.
She's fair as my sister and I were,
when we sat still and felt our mother's
skillful hands tugging at our scalps
as she wove the fine, flaxen strands
into ropes hanging down our backs.
Her fingers read our hair like Braille.
We gave up braiding early,
preferring the ponytail.

But this girl, the room's darkness
dissolving in her hair's pale sheen,
knows the strength of a three-fold cord.
From three, her hands weave one.
From the flood past her waist, she crafts
a channel; from the field, she hews a furrow.
Serenely, her fingers move through segments,
each twist a call to order she's answered.

The Saint of Inner Light

Paul Klee (1921)

The tram winds up the mountain
like a mythical beast, groaning
as its tail separates at the hinges
from the rest of its body.
The peak awaits me.
A bakery advertises itself with a six-
foot plaster loaf of bread, a wonder
to the child across the aisle.
As we climb the hill, the houses grow.
Clouds part, it will be a blue day.
I'm boat-eyed, large-nosed, ambiguous.

Zürich, Switzerland, 2012

Nocturne

I want to attend to the evening:
to impress on memory these roses,
unruly pink climbers, disheveled white,
the bee-strung, heavy-haired lavender
planted between bushes for eye's ease—
the endless rung of moment after moment,
of rose-breath and globes of wild onion.
So many years I lived without paying attention.
It was all boys and makeup and pop charts.
Maybe I wasted the beauty around me
because it still gleamed in my round cheeks.
Maybe my thick and shining braids bound me.
Grace withdrew from my distracted gaze.
Now that I lament, it's easier to praise
a promise that won't word itself—
the bush of half-bloomed, ghost-streaked
red roses offering at each angle
withered petals alongside sumptuous ruffles.

The Strawberry Moon

In Europe, it's called the rose moon
or the honey moon, but in America,
the Algonquins named the June full moon
after the ripeness of strawberries
that occurs at its rise, the cusp of summer.
Through a trick of light, it *does* shine pink,
but paler pink than strawberries, more the sheer
pink of vintage tulle or lingerie lace.
It's considered good luck to marry beneath one.
As I change for bed in the darkened room,
the moon's the whispery pink of my lips,
pink of the rose quartz earrings I unlatch.
I anticipate my husband's day-heavy body,
how he'll curl his legs around me so that we,
too, form a globe, my legs tucked within his.
As sleep ripples down like a handful of roses,
may our dreams be as honey-gold and sweet
in our memory as the strawberries we picked
and ate impatiently in the fields, fruit pulpy
red beneath its three-fold leaves.

Ghost Wife

In Chinese folk tradition, the ghost wife is a deceased unmarried woman who is symbolically married to a living man in order to give her a lineage.

I chose him when I turned eighteen,
though an early death had intervened.
He picked my bag of clothes up from the curb.
His wife did not object: at the wedding,
they burned me a paper ring and Mercedes.
Now, I'm always fed, have a home and kin.
At the Ghost Festival, they reserve me a chair
for dinner and set a lit lantern boat afloat
beneath the full moon so I won't get lost.
In return, I protect my adopted children,
help them with exams and recess bullies.
The earth is crammed and breathing.
I stride the winds freely, eat *Cao Zai Guo,*
steamed tortoise green for the dead.

Waking Poem for Andy

Sometimes, I wake at night from fear
of the short time I've been given here.
But then, relieved, I turn and hear
your breathing on my pillow, a clear
sign there's nothing on earth severe
enough to have rendered me less dear.
And though our life does not appear
to others as ideal, if the sheer
horror of illness scares them, we're
not concerned. Let them disappear
from our world; they won't interfere,
my love. You'll take me at my nadir,
someday, and let death's flame sear
you. But not yet, dear God, not this year.

Church of St. Prex

Marianne von Werefkin (1914)

She wasn't afraid of bold colors,
and loved especially autumn's orange and gold,
red trees ripe for wind, yellow bunches
leafing over St. Prex's purple steeple.

Though I'm bound by words and pen,
I often find myself longing for a line
of poetry to wrack itself against my paper
like a streak of carmine against the white,

to write past the dull sheen of my days
the way the painter gleaned her vivid hues
from German twilight and afternoons—
October a martyr, pitched towards the fire.

Migrations

I want to find meaning
in the birds' hypnotic
sweeps from lawn to tree.
The sudden way they lift
together, black shawls,
gales of rusties squalling
from branch to branch.
I seek a purpose
beyond hibernation,
food, and breeding.
I want myth and prophecy.
I want my father
to rise from death
and speak to me.

Grackles

Grackles aren't granted a term as lilting
as *murmuration*, starlings' mellifluous tides.
Grackles are simply grackles,
plain squawkers not lined with crimson,
or graced with the petite charm of the chickadee.
They're commuters on the migratory subway.
Ordinary birds, thrift shop birds,
last-season's shoes and pocketbook birds.
Even their name brings to mind swollen ankles.
My grandmother, stout and Russian,
was a grackle, not a swift or starling.
She walked everywhere with purpose, bickered,
ate bread and buttered cabbage for dinner.
I come from a lineage of grackles.
So it's no wonder that the birds gather
in my front yard, noisy fliers, survivors,
hundreds of them wind-slapped
in their common, rapturous clouds.

Sparrow

When my son shouts, "Bird in the house!"
I don't believe him, till the frightened sparrow
wheels through the hall, thrashing against windows.
In a mad dance, a triple-time Strauss, it waltzes
and dips from room to room, brown whirlwind
of feathered panic, bashing pane after pane.
I try to fling a sheet over its whippet-quick
body, but all I catch is sun and dust.
Finally, it rests on a floor lamp's perch.
No time to waste—I close the door, open
the nearest window, wait for it to flee.
And it does, to my son's glee, in a snap.
Through a gap in the oak, it disappears
toward the horizon, into all that blue.

IV

Secrets of Ferns

Anselm Kiefer (1996–2000)

The secrets of ferns
wear little white nightgowns.
They float like ghost-moths.
Stars with sleeves,
full of dreaming.
The ferns subdue
their green at night.
But they still have it,
this green, hidden.
My out-breaths ascend
as my lungs empty.
All the dreams
of all the sleepers
merge, little bits floating
over every continent.
All the dreams
become one enormous dream
and the secrets, one secret,
larger than the earth.

Blue Slippers

Cobalt velvet, cornflower bows,
I lace them to spirit feet.
Words unfurl behind each step.
I'm followed by a ribbon of script.
Here's my letter to you, beak-born
by the Lady of Grey Days.
Bluebirds come to her grey-eyed call.
All the words I won't say,
I dance from my tender arches.
The letter goes on for days and days.
It will reach you forever.
It will find you in ten thousand years.

Table by the Window

It's time to pour the tea.
I've opened the windows,
despite the snow thistling
the rooftops. The teapot's
fat as a hand-fed rabbit.
I've set the table with yellow roses,
one for each kiss for your arrival.
The door waits to hear your tread.
I linger at the bedroom mirror,
my fingers freesias itching to flower.

Bedroom With Open Door

It's ten thirty. One lamp gleams
beside the window's green curtain.
I've wound the clock; its pinecones
hang beside each other, a couple
asleep in their heavy bed.
The front door's open. The clove-
like scent of carnations has settled
in corners like a cat by the vents.
Every half hour, a wooden bird chirps.
I've trussed its glass eyes.
I won't tell you which books
I've placed on my nightstand. Guess.

Epithalamium

The muck of rain and leaves slick on logs,
swollen, split-open, layered pastry of rot.
Hanging above, twisted around themselves,
twine hundred-year-old wisteria vines,
ropey fishbone braids bare of blossom,
swinging over puddles and the nested tangle
of needles and forest detritus that shelter
mice and lure the eager noses of dogs.
Imagine the vines in spring, their fragrance
almost profane in its shameless sweetness.
Though even now, the two vines wrap
around each other, inseparable, single,
waiting for sun and heat to force
from them that wanton purple cry.

For Andy

Blue Hydrangeas

The way they shade from milky celadon
to indigo, the summer afternoon blue
of them, grounded tugged-down cumuli.
Their swaggery mob-cap profusion,
the generosity with which one or two
will fill a vase with hue and height.
For how they bundle in sea-wind,
suburban garden, neglected park.
Both elegant and humble, armful
of lace-trimmed lingerie or tulle.
Even the autumn hulls of them,
how tenderly they wither to sepia.
For all these reasons, I stand at the window
and watch my neighbor's hydrangeas
in June, full-flower moon blossom,
all of me alive, sun-sluiced and glad.

To the Man Who Yelled "Hey, Baby!" At Me

Yes, you, in the smashed up swerving Camaro
(not knowing you were driving my seventeen
year-old self's dream car), you have a lot of nerve.
I know it's Friday, and the weekend's a bar tab
you haven't yet opened, but I'm your mother's age.
Still, "Hey, Baby!" is a classic, and so's the white
tee you were wearing, from the glimpse I got,
and it's hot enough this November for shorts,
which puts anyone in a sportive mood.
You were rude, no doubt, and your male privilege,
on principle, offends me (I'm old enough
to be called *ma'am*, and you jamming the brakes).
Still, on balance, you put some bounce in the balls
of my feet, and really, it was kind of sweet,
a little treat for my day, a little heat and flounce.

Prom Dresses

When I was in high school, I could still find
1950s gowns in thrift shops, Simplicity patterns
pinched in the waist but with skirts voluminous
as Christmas trees, layers of chiffon and tulle.
Baby pink, ice blue, sea foam: cocktail colors.
They were the prettiest dresses I'd ever seen.
By the time I reached senior year, 1986,
the hues were brighter and the parties wilder.
My Gunne Sax still hangs in my closet, ecru lace.
I can shimmy into it, almost zipper it shut,
though not quite, and anyway, it was designed
for an unlined face and hair without grey.
Our prom theme was "Forever Young," the fantasy
my friends and I had of how beautiful and unharmed
we'd remain. Slow dances, leaning on boys'
shoulders, the engraved flutes of ginger ale.

Woman in a Green Dress

Tonight, I'll emerge as an emerald,
cat's eye, split peeled kiwi.

Christmas fir, hung with lights.
I want a fake fur shawl and kitten heels.

Spray my hair up on the big rollers.
Shellac my nails Big Apple.

Scratch under my age, I'm still young,
in love with girlhood and prospect.

Trim that dress low, off the shoulder,
sheen around my hips, seamed hose.

I'm a bower, rosemary, cockatoo.
Dances conjure in my shoes.

The Tightrope Walker

Jean-Louis Forain (c. 1885)

Almost no one watches her.
She unnerves the audience
as she perches on the wire,
each flex and gyration a gasp.
Nor does she glance at the crowd
of top hats and bonnets beneath her.
Her gaze fixes above the others' heads
as she cradles a pole for balance.
How taut she must keep herself,
how supple and fraught each breath,
to avoid even the slightest misstep.
She knows her limits, flaunts them.
Her red stockings rebuke caution.
A black band circles her throat.
She braces for the right moment
to trust the tension, and leap.

How to Hula Hoop

Love the ridiculous.
Fear not contortions of the body
nor the vibrations of failure.
Place the hoop on your waist
where your husband puts his hands.
Then gyrate like crazy.
There's no single method:
make of your hips a swivel stool
and your pelvis a pendulum.
Some will spiral slowly,
letting the hoop rock and swing
like a carousel of pastel horses.
I, graceless, whirl myself wildly
from abdomen to knees.
Normally, the hoop tumbles
down my legs in two minutes
or three—but occasionally,
it will stay and settle,
and I'll sway like a cartoon snake
in a basket, lifting my arms
above my head, seductive Salome.
Or rather, a middle-aged woman
with her moments briefly balanced,
a car wheel going nowhere,
and in no special hurry to get there.

Late Summer

August evening, church bells,
light shattered on the quick
creek as in a Seurat painting,
grass thick with Queen Anne's lace,
the summer sun still so late
in setting that bedtime comes late
to the children scattered in the garden.
Late summer, and the roses in second
bloom know what's coming.
But for now, bells, water, laughter,
my mother and I walking together
arm in arm, because happiness
is a decision each of us has made,
without even discussing it.

A Briar

pierced her breast.
It bore into her sternum,
then wound through her lungs,
its little thorns pricking
the sleeves of her breath.
She tried to reach her hand
down her throat to yank
the branch out of her mouth,
but it held fast to her rib
cage, had calcified
into bone, inseparable cane
and leaf. At times,
the briar caused her to cough,
or slashed her chest muscles
till her body spasmed in pain.
But at other times,
it paused in its windings.
Occasionally, it put forth
blossoms as big as saucers,
claret roses of petal on petal,
for which, grateful, she wept.

August

The small pink rose
by the castle gate
glows in the twilight,
gathering strands
of sunset in its petals.
The tower's a ruin.
But I keep my eye on the rose,
on its many-hooded gaze
that doesn't turn away
from what approaches.
To bloom is so foolish
that it must be wisdom.

Acknowledgements

Anglican Theological Review: "The Ploughman"

Atticus Review: "Cape May at Dusk," "How to Hula Hoop," "Blue Hydrangeas," "To the Man Who Yelled 'Hey Baby' At Me"

Christian Century: "Psalm 137 for Noah"

Conversing with Cancer: "Something Understood"

The Cresset: "The Secret of Ferns"

Five Points: "Girl Braiding Her Hair," "Nocturne," "Instructions," "To a Healthy Friend"

Image: "Ya-Quddus," "Fisherman," "Salter," "Birdcatcher," "Merchant"

Peacock Journal: "Return," "Blue Slippers," "Epithalamium," "Late Summer," "August"

Poet Lore: "Grackles"

Rock & Sling: "First Advent" (as "Winter Burial") and "Christmas Eve" (as "Oh, Little Town of Bethlehem")

Saint Katherine Review: "Holy Saturday, 1945," "Lenten Crocuses," "Poetry Belongs to the Dying," "A Walk in November"

Smartish Pace: "A Briar," "Department Meeting," "Ghost Wife"

Southern Poetry Review: "Kharkov, 1933"

Specs Journal: "Third Advent" (as "Advent")

Terminus: "A Boy Stands Up During Supper," "The Empty Tomb," "Paul Klee, The Saint of Inner Light"

Whale Road Review: "Inauguration"

Windhover: "Second Advent," "Eating Baklava on New Year's Eve"

Epigraph by Anna Kamieńska from "A Prayer That Will Be Answered," trans. Grażyna Drabik and David Curzon.

Acknowledgements

"Sometimes A Boy Stands Up During Supper": from Rilke's "Sometimes A Man Stands Up During Supper" ("Manchmal Steht Einer Auf Bein Abendbrot").

"The Wild Swan Geese": Swan Geese live primarily in Russia and China. The poem was inspired by a Russian fairy tale called "The Wild Swan Geese." The image of the rotten piano is taken from Else Lasker-Schüler's poem "My Blue Piano" ("Mein blaues Klavier").

"Something Understood": The title is the last line of George Herbert's poem "Prayer (I)."

"Es Wird Schon Glei Dumpa" is an Austrian Christmas carol popular in German-speaking countries. It is written in Austrian dialect, and the title translates to "It will soon be dark."

"The Secret of Ferns" is based on a series of paintings by Anselm Kiefer, which are inspired by a Paul Celan poem of the same name. ("Geheimnis der Farne")

"The Colloquy" is a 10th-11th century grammatical primer written in Anglo Saxon and Latin by the English abbot Ælfric. Its purpose was to teach boys how to read Latin. The *Colloquy* consists of a series of dialogues between a "teacher" or "master" and members of various professions, in which artisans, farmers, fishermen, and others explain to the children what they do in their daily lives. The text gives a detailed depiction of life at the time, and also embeds spiritual lessons within its practical lessons. I am indebted to Anne Watkins for her translation of Ælfric's *Colloquy* from Latin into English. I have made some slight changes to her translations by referring to the original Anglo Saxon text.

With thanks to my sisters in the metastatic and inflammatory breast cancer communities, who understand this difficult life, especially the Beach House women—Kate Strosser, Ginny Mason, Brenda Denzler, Kim Alexander, Lin Blank Bell—and Terry Lynn Arnold. Memory eternal to those whom the world has lost since the publication of my last book, including Kate Strosser, Holli Durkin, Julie Caples, Ishiuan Hargrove, Maria Roark, Billie Clemens, Kay Byer, and anyone who has died since this book went to press.

Thank you also to Dr. Linda Hendricks and the nurses and staff at Central Georgia Cancer Care for your patient and kind care, and for always viewing me as a whole person.

Acknowledgements

Thank you to my poet friends, who have encouraged me and critiqued my work: Sara Hughes, Jennifer Franklin, Julie Moore, Barbara Crooker, Tania Runyan, Jill Baumgaertner, Kathryn Stripling Byer, and Nicole Cooley.

Deep gratitude to Don Martin and to the editors and staff at Cascade Press for working with me and for publishing this book. I can't express my appreciation enough, especially for Don's meticulous editing of the poems.

With great love to my mother, sister and late father, my beloved family, my source of joy and comfort.

And to my husband Andy and son Noah: everything, everything, everything, always.

"He will swallow up death for all time,
And the Lord God will wipe tears away from all faces."
—Isaiah 25:8

COLLECTIONS IN THIS SERIES INCLUDE:

Made in the USA
Middletown, DE
13 August 2018